I0813315

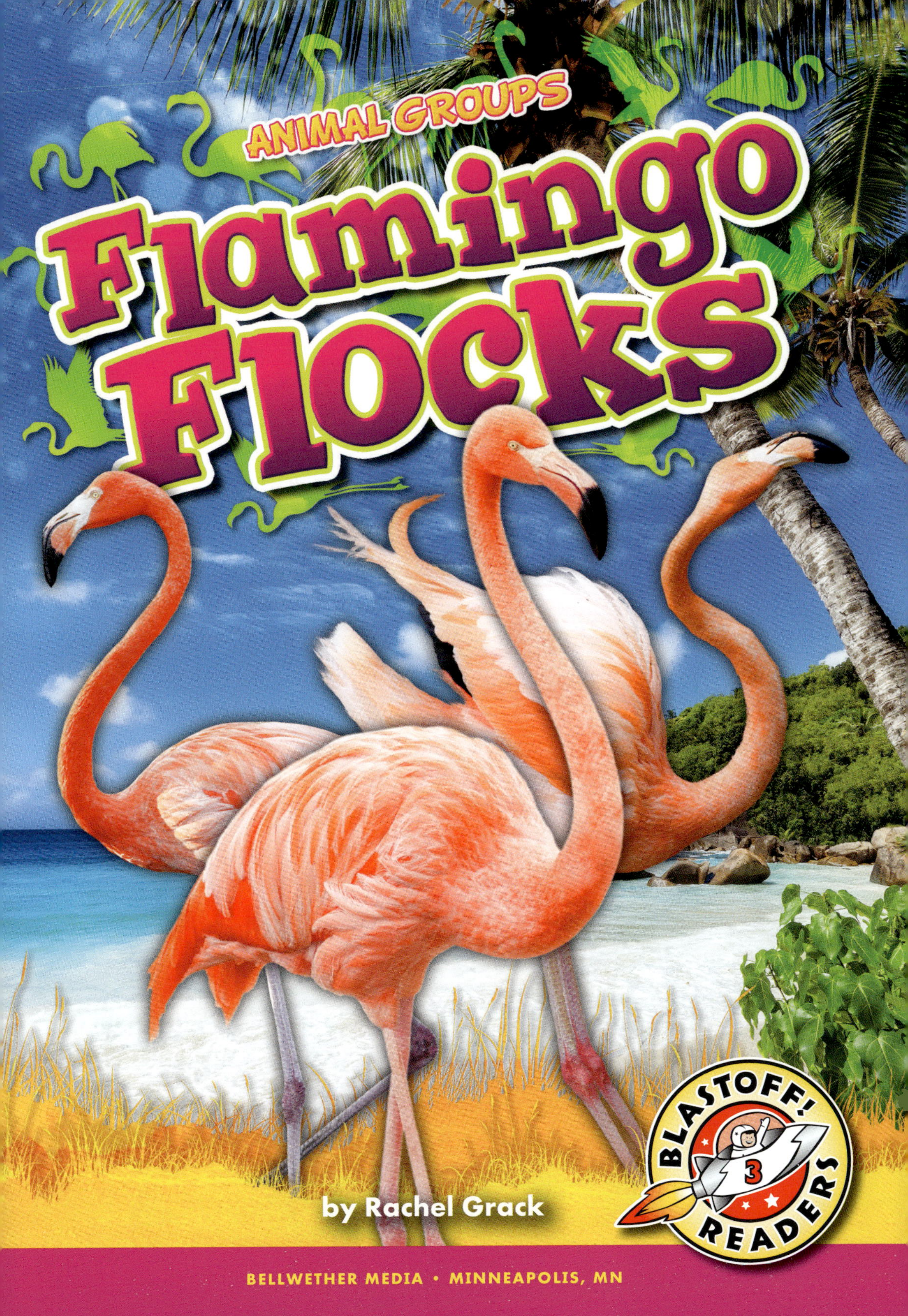
ANIMAL GROUPS
Flamingo Flocks
by Rachel Grack
BLASTOFF! 3 READERS
BELLWETHER MEDIA • MINNEAPOLIS, MN

Blastoff! Readers are carefully developed by literacy experts to build reading stamina and move students toward fluency by combining standards-based content with developmentally appropriate text.

Level 1 provides the most support through repetition of high-frequency words, light text, predictable sentence patterns, and strong visual support.

Level 2 offers early readers a bit more challenge through varied sentences, increased text load, and text-supportive special features.

Level 3 advances early-fluent readers toward fluency through increased text load, less reliance on photos, advancing concepts, longer sentences, and more complex special features.

Reading Level

Grade K

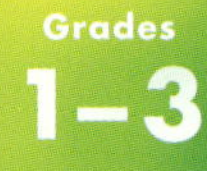

Grades 1–3

Grade 4

This edition first published in 2026 by Bellwether Media, Inc.

Library of Congress Cataloging-in-Publication Data

LC record for Flamingo Flocks available at: https://lccn.loc.gov/2025018605

Editor: Suzane Nguyen Designer: Brittany McIntosh

Printed in the United States of America, North Mankato, MN.

Table of Contents

Standout Birds

flamboyance

Flamingos are **tropical** birds. Their bright feathers stand out! There are six different kinds of flamingos.

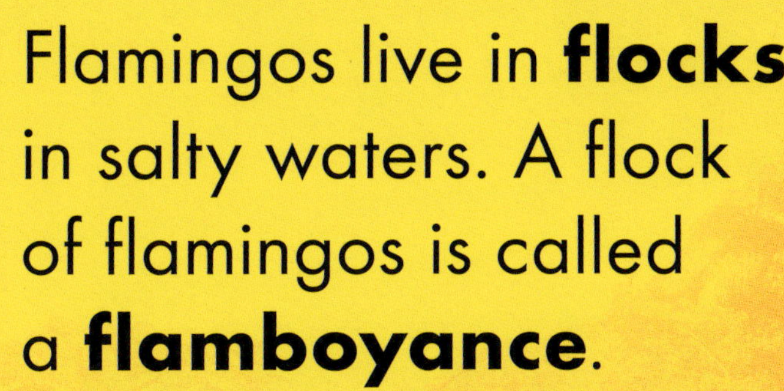

Flamingos live in **flocks** in salty waters. A flock of flamingos is called a **flamboyance**.

N
W E
S

range =

Flock Life

Flamingos live in big groups. A flamboyance can have thousands of birds.

Flamingos eat, **preen**, and rest together. They can form long-lasting friendships with one another.

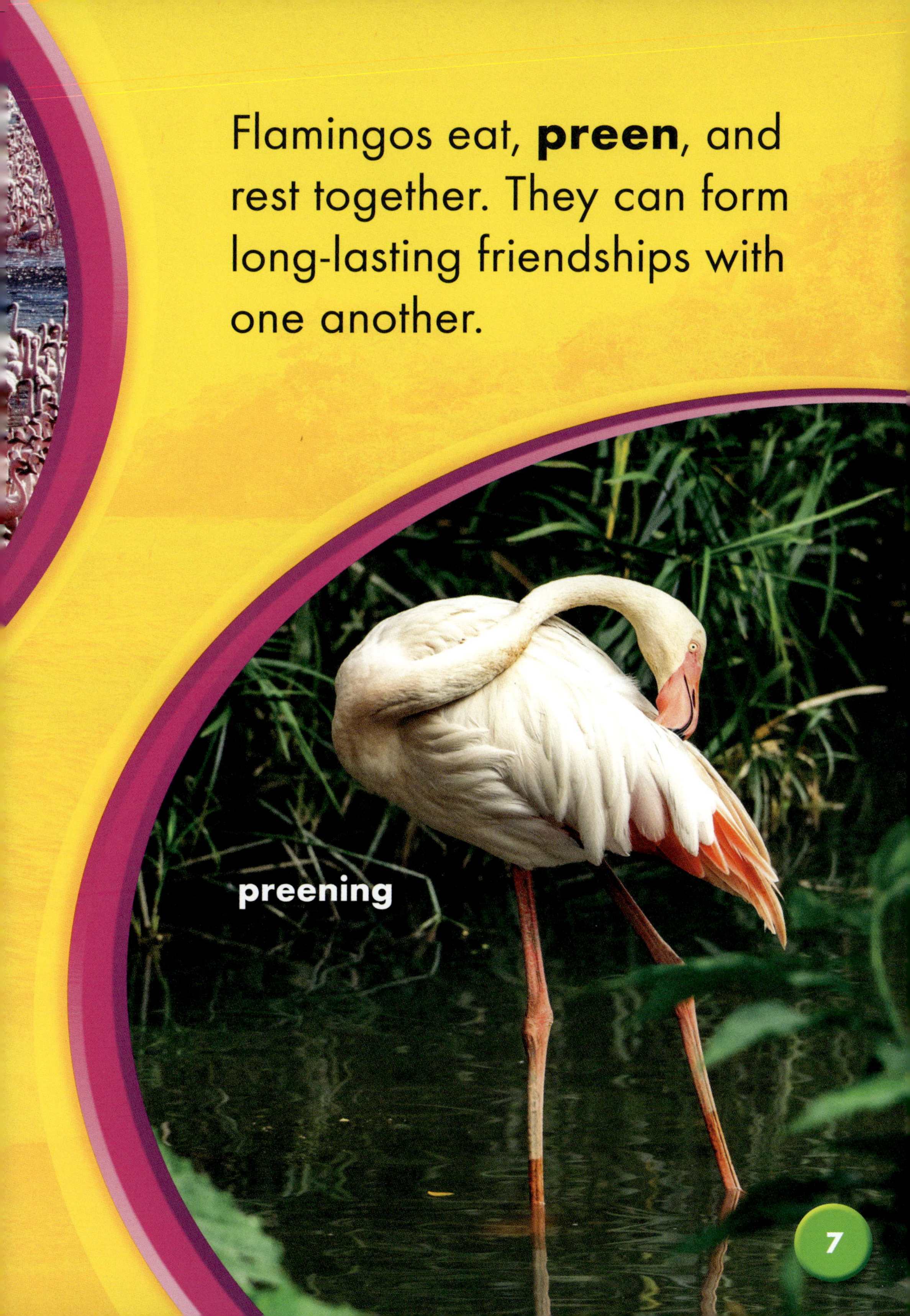

preening

Flamingos are noisy birds. They make different sounds to **communicate**. When angry, flamingos growl and grunt.

Loud honks and growls warn the flock of danger. Some honks keep the flock together while flying.

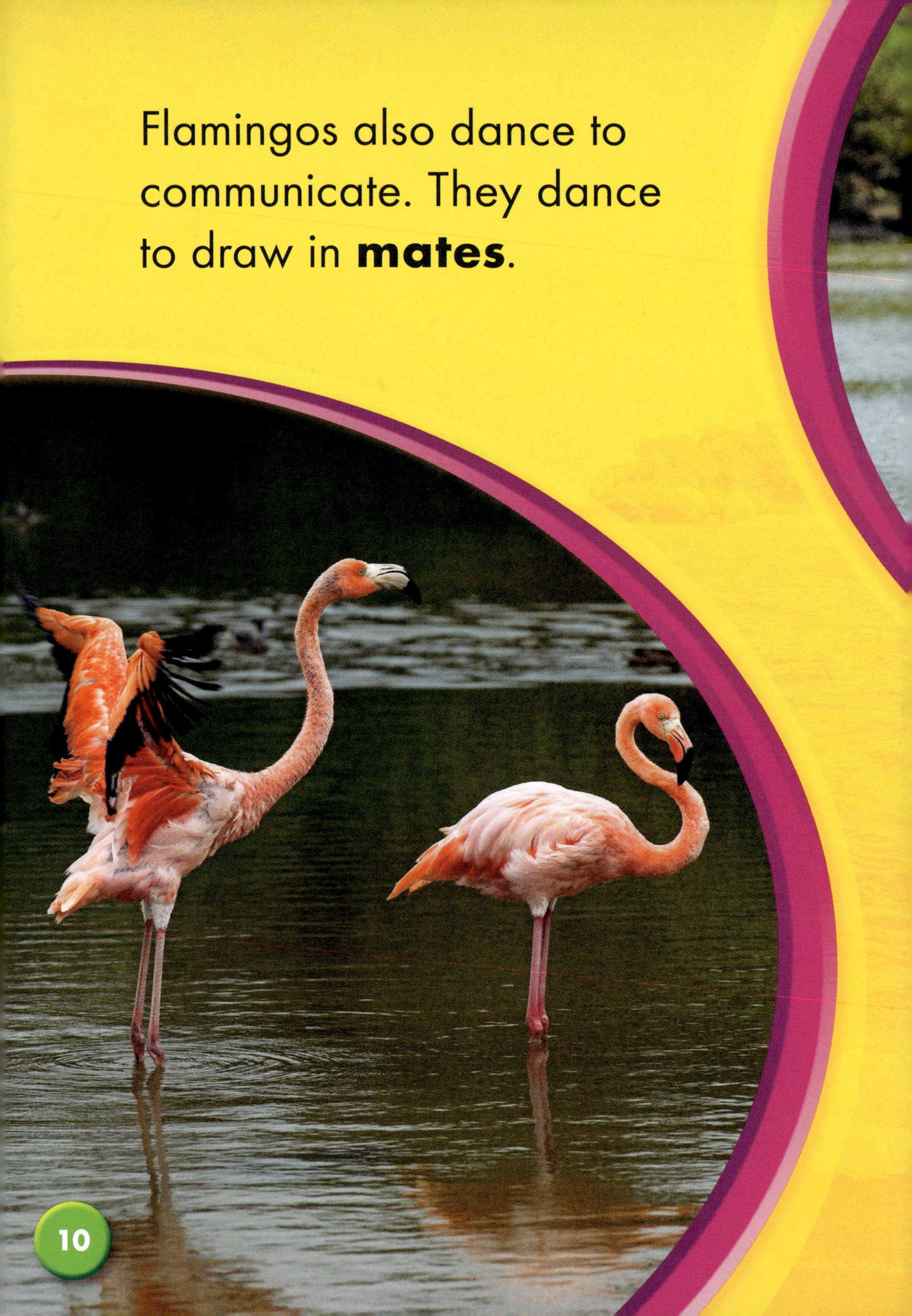

Flamingos also dance to communicate. They dance to draw in **mates**.

flamingo mating dance

Flamingos stretch their necks and spread their wings. Flocks will even march together! Then flamingos pair up with their favorite dancer.

Food and Friends

Adult flamingos have few **predators**. But some animals hunt them. Large birds feed on eggs and **chicks**.

Flocks spend much of their time in water. They stay in large groups to keep safe.

Flamingos eat shrimp, fly **larvae**, and **algae**. Some foods make their feathers turn pink, red, or orange.

To find food, flamingos shovel up mud with their **bills**. Their comblike teeth remove the mud and leave the food.

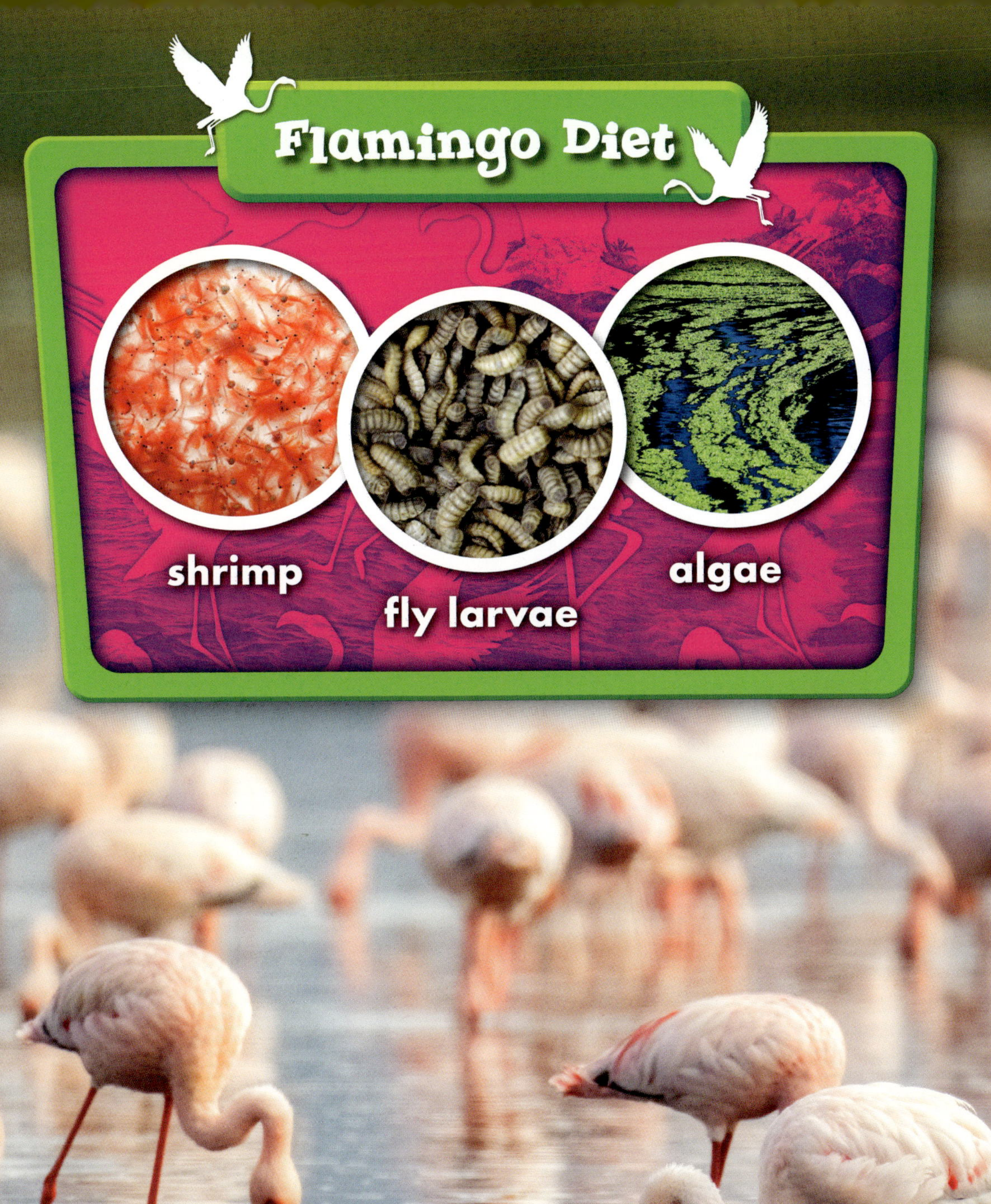
Flamingo Diet
shrimp
fly larvae
algae

Flamingos live in the same groups for life. They form friendships with other flamingos who help them find food.

Flock friends also guard each other's nests and chicks. They keep young safe from harm.

Raising Chicks

Flamingos build tall nests with mud in **shallow** waters. Nests keep eggs cool and dry.

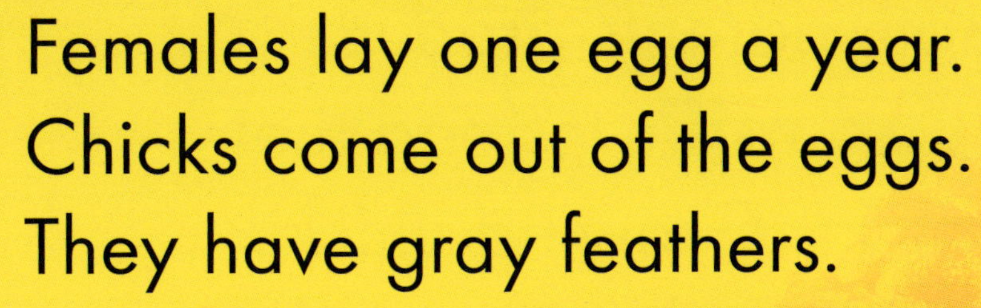

Females lay one egg a year.
Chicks come out of the eggs.
They have gray feathers.

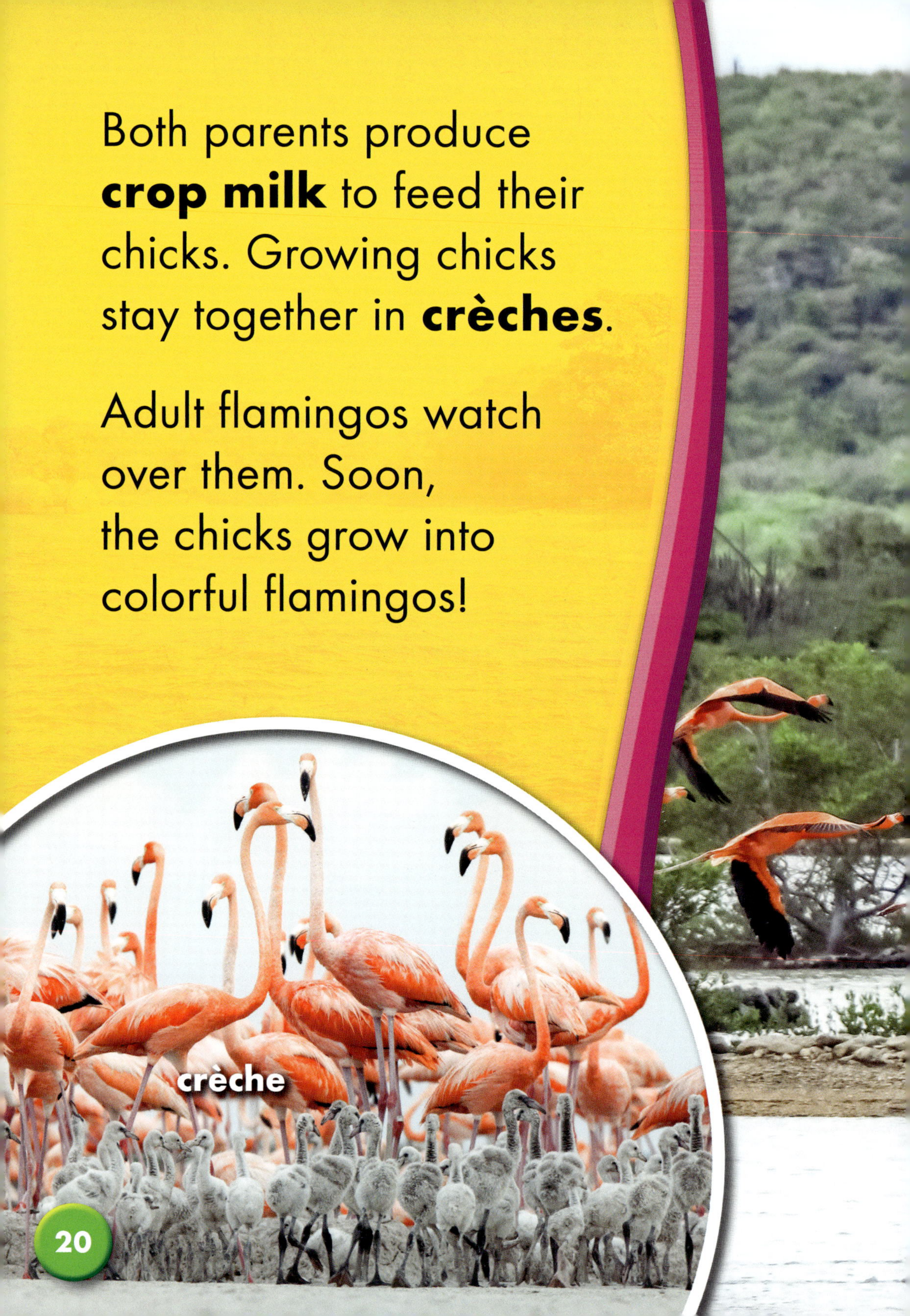

Both parents produce **crop milk** to feed their chicks. Growing chicks stay together in **crèches**.

Adult flamingos watch over them. Soon, the chicks grow into colorful flamingos!

Glossary

algae—plants and plantlike living things; most kinds of algae grow in water.

bills—the mouths of birds

chicks—baby flamingos

communicate—to share thoughts and feelings using sounds, faces, and actions

crèches—groups of flamingo chicks that are cared for by adult flamingos

crop milk—a liquid similar to milk that is made by adult flamingos to feed chicks

flamboyance—a flock of flamingos

flocks—groups of birds

larvae—baby insects that have come from eggs; larvae look like worms.

mates—a pair of adult animals that produce offspring

predators—animals that hunt other animals for food

preen—to use the bill to clean feathers

shallow—not deep

tropical—related to places that are hot and humid

To Learn More

AT THE LIBRARY

Murray, Julie. *Flamingos.* Minneapolis, Minn.: Abdo Kids, 2023.

Riggs, Kate. *Flamingos.* Mankato, Minn.: The Creative Company, 2023.

Rose, Rachel. *Flamingo.* Minneapolis, Minn.: Bearport Publishing, 2025.

ON THE WEB

FACTSURFER

Factsurfer.com gives you a safe, fun way to find more information.

1. Go to www.factsurfer.com.
2. Enter "flamingo flocks" into the search box and click 🔍.
3. Select your book cover to see a list of related content.

Index

The images in this book are reproduced through the courtesy of: Sanit Fuangnakhon, front cover (left flamingo, right flamingo), p. 17 (left); ILYA AKINSHIN, front cover (middle flamingo), p. 3; Lucky-photographer, front cover (background); VanWyckExpress, p. 4; Smileus, p. 4 (inset); John Warburton-Lee Photography/ Alamy Stock Photo, p. 6; Nik Hisham, p. 7; Pascale Gueret, pp. 8-9; Sergey Uryadnikov, p. 9; GFC Collection/ Alamy Stock Photo, p. 10; William Mullins/ Alamy Stock Photo, p. 11; Stephaniellen, p. 12; pornpoj, p. 13; delmapto, p. 14; KenCanning, pp. 14-15; Tree Vongvitavat, p. 15 (shrimp); Ivan M. Quijano, p. 15 (fly larvae); Alexlky, p. 15 (algae); Gary Peplow, p. 16; cyo bo, p. 17 (right); val lawless, p. 18; Asmus Koefoed, p. 19; Nature Picture Library/ Alamy Stock Photo, p. 20; Gail Johnson, pp. 20-21; Potapov Alexander, p. 23.